ANARCHIST COOKBOOK
Recipe

Date:

Ingredients

Directions

Notes

ANARCHIST COOKBOOK

Recipe

Date:

Ingredients

Directions

Notes

ANARCHIST COOKBOOK
Recipe

Date:

Ingredients

Directions

Notes

ANARCHIST COOKBOOK
Recipe

Date:

Ingredients

Directions

Notes

ANARCHIST COOKBOOK

Recipe

Date:

Ingredients

Directions

Notes

ANARCHIST COOKBOOK
Recipe

Date:

Ingredients

Directions

Notes

ANARCHIST COOKBOOK
Recipe

Date:

Ingredients

Directions

Notes

ANARCHIST COOKBOOK

Recipe

Date:

Ingredients

Directions

Notes

ANARCHIST COOKBOOK

Recipe

Date:

Ingredients

Directions

Notes

ANARCHIST COOKBOOK

Recipe

Date:

Ingredients

Directions

Notes

ANARCHIST COOKBOOK
Recipe

Date:

Ingredients

Directions

Notes

ANARCHIST COOKBOOK
Recipe

Date:

Ingredients

Directions

Notes

ANARCHIST COOKBOOK
Recipe

Date:

Ingredients

Directions

Notes

ANARCHIST COOKBOOK

Recipe

Date:

Ingredients

Directions

Notes

ANARCHIST COOKBOOK
Recipe

Date:

Ingredients

Directions

Notes

ANARCHIST COOKBOOK

Recipe

Date:

Ingredients

Directions

Notes

ANARCHIST COOKBOOK
Recipe

Date:

Ingredients

Directions

Notes

ANARCHIST COOKBOOK

Recipe

Date:

Ingredients

Directions

Notes

ANARCHIST COOKBOOK
Recipe

Date:

Ingredients

Directions

Notes

ANARCHIST COOKBOOK
Recipe

Date:

Ingredients

Directions

Notes

ANARCHIST COOKBOOK
Recipe

Date:

Ingredients

Directions

Notes

ANARCHIST COOKBOOK
Recipe

Date:

Ingredients

Directions

Notes

ANARCHIST COOKBOOK
Recipe

Date:

Ingredients

Directions

Notes

ANARCHIST COOKBOOK

Recipe

Date:

Ingredients

Directions

Notes

ANARCHIST COOKBOOK
Recipe

Date:

Ingredients

Directions

Notes

ANARCHIST COOKBOOK
Recipe

Date:

Ingredients

Directions

Notes

ANARCHIST COOKBOOK
Recipe

Date:

Ingredients

Directions

Notes

ANARCHIST COOKBOOK
Recipe

Date:

Ingredients

Directions

Notes

ANARCHIST COOKBOOK
Recipe

Date:

Ingredients

Directions

Notes

ANARCHIST COOKBOOK
Recipe

Date:

Ingredients

Directions

Notes

ANARCHIST COOKBOOK

Recipe

Date:

Ingredients

Directions

Notes

ANARCHIST COOKBOOK
Recipe

Date:

Ingredients

Directions

Notes

ANARCHIST COOKBOOK
Recipe

Date:

Ingredients

Directions

Notes

ANARCHIST COOKBOOK

Recipe

Date:

Ingredients

Directions

Notes

ANARCHIST COOKBOOK
Recipe

Date:

Ingredients

Directions

Notes

ANARCHIST COOKBOOK

Recipe

Date:

Ingredients

Directions

Notes

ANARCHIST COOKBOOK
Recipe

Date:

Ingredients

Directions

Notes

ANARCHIST COOKBOOK
Recipe

Date:

Ingredients

Directions

Notes

ANARCHIST COOKBOOK
Recipe

Date:

Ingredients

Directions

Notes

ANARCHIST COOKBOOK
Recipe

Date:

Ingredients

Directions

Notes

ANARCHIST COOKBOOK
Recipe

Date:

Ingredients

Directions

Notes

ANARCHIST COOKBOOK
Recipe

Date:

Ingredients

Directions

Notes

ANARCHIST COOKBOOK
Recipe

Date:

Ingredients

Directions

Notes

ANARCHIST COOKBOOK

Recipe

Date:

Ingredients

Directions

Notes

ANARCHIST COOKBOOK
Recipe

Date:

Ingredients

Directions

Notes

ANARCHIST COOKBOOK
Recipe

Date:

Ingredients

Directions

Notes

ANARCHIST COOKBOOK
Recipe

Date:

Ingredients

Directions

Notes

ANARCHIST COOKBOOK
Recipe

Date:

Ingredients

Directions

Notes

ANARCHIST COOKBOOK

Recipe

Date:

Ingredients

Directions

Notes

ANARCHIST COOKBOOK
Recipe

Date:

Ingredients

Directions

Notes

ANARCHIST COOKBOOK
Recipe

Date:

Ingredients

Directions

Notes

ANARCHIST COOKBOOK
Recipe

Date:

Ingredients

Directions

Notes

ANARCHIST COOKBOOK
Recipe

Date:

Ingredients

Directions

Notes

ANARCHIST COOKBOOK
Recipe

Date:

Ingredients

Directions

Notes

ANARCHIST COOKBOOK
Recipe

Date:

Ingredients

Directions

Notes

ANARCHIST COOKBOOK
Recipe

Date:

Ingredients

Directions

Notes

ANARCHIST COOKBOOK
Recipe

Date:

Ingredients

Directions

Notes

ANARCHIST COOKBOOK
Recipe

Date:

Ingredients

Directions

Notes

ANARCHIST COOKBOOK
Recipe

Date:

Ingredients

Directions

Notes

ANARCHIST COOKBOOK
Recipe

Date:

Ingredients

Directions

Notes

ANARCHIST COOKBOOK
Recipe

Date:

Ingredients

Directions

Notes

ANARCHIST COOKBOOK
Recipe

Date:

Ingredients

Directions

Notes

ANARCHIST COOKBOOK
Recipe

Date:

Ingredients

Directions

Notes

ANARCHIST COOKBOOK

Recipe

Date:

Ingredients

Directions

Notes

ANARCHIST COOKBOOK
Recipe

Date:

Ingredients

Directions

Notes

ANARCHIST COOKBOOK
Recipe

Date:

Ingredients

Directions

Notes

ANARCHIST COOKBOOK
Recipe

Date:

Ingredients

Directions

Notes

ANARCHIST COOKBOOK
Recipe

Date:

Ingredients

Directions

Notes

ANARCHIST COOKBOOK
Recipe

Date:

Ingredients

Directions

Notes

ANARCHIST COOKBOOK

Recipe

Date:

Ingredients

Directions

Notes

ANARCHIST COOKBOOK
Recipe

Date:

Ingredients

Directions

Notes

ANARCHIST COOKBOOK
Recipe

Date:

Ingredients

Directions

Notes

ANARCHIST COOKBOOK
Recipe

Date:

Ingredients

Directions

Notes

ANARCHIST COOKBOOK
Recipe

Date:

Ingredients

Directions

Notes

ANARCHIST COOKBOOK
Recipe

Date:

Ingredients

Directions

Notes

ANARCHIST COOKBOOK
Recipe

Date:

Ingredients

Directions

Notes

ANARCHIST COOKBOOK
Recipe

Date:

Ingredients

Directions

Notes

ANARCHIST COOKBOOK
Recipe

Date:

Ingredients

Directions

Notes

ANARCHIST COOKBOOK
Recipe

Date:

Ingredients

Directions

Notes

ANARCHIST COOKBOOK
Recipe

Date:

Ingredients

Directions

Notes

ANARCHIST COOKBOOK
Recipe

Date:

Ingredients

Directions

Notes

ANARCHIST COOKBOOK
Recipe

Date:

Ingredients

Directions

Notes

ANARCHIST COOKBOOK
Recipe

Date:

Ingredients

Directions

Notes

ANARCHIST COOKBOOK
Recipe

Date:

Ingredients

Directions

Notes

ANARCHIST COOKBOOK

Recipe

Date:

Ingredients

Directions

Notes

ANARCHIST COOKBOOK
Recipe

Date:

Ingredients

Directions

Notes

ANARCHIST COOKBOOK
Recipe

Date:

Ingredients

Directions

Notes

ANARCHIST COOKBOOK
Recipe

Date:

Ingredients

Directions

Notes

ANARCHIST COOKBOOK
Recipe

Date:

Ingredients

Directions

Notes

ANARCHIST COOKBOOK
Recipe

Date:

Ingredients

Directions

Notes

ANARCHIST COOKBOOK
Recipe

Date:

Ingredients

Directions

Notes

ANARCHIST COOKBOOK

Recipe

Date:

Ingredients

Directions

Notes

ANARCHIST COOKBOOK
Recipe

Date:

Ingredients

Directions

Notes

ANARCHIST COOKBOOK
Recipe

Date:

Ingredients

Directions

Notes

ANARCHIST COOKBOOK
Recipe

Date:

Ingredients

Directions

Notes

ANARCHIST COOKBOOK
Recipe

Date:

Ingredients

Directions

Notes

ANARCHIST COOKBOOK
Recipe

Date:

Ingredients

Directions

Notes

ANARCHIST COOKBOOK

Recipe

Date:

Ingredients

Directions

Notes

ANARCHIST COOKBOOK
Recipe

Date:

Ingredients

Directions

Notes

www.ingramcontent.com/pod-product-compliance
Lightning Source LLC
Chambersburg PA
CBHW080422290526
45791CB00008BA/2384